SLOW THE
FUCK DOWN

30 REASONS WHY YOUR JOY MATTERS MORE THAN YOUR TO-DO LIST

ASHLEY LOOKER

Ashley Looker
3807 N. Gove St.
Tacoma, WA 98407

Ordering Information:
Quantity sales. Special discounts are available on quantity purchases
by corporations, associations, and others. For details, contact the
"Special Sales Department" at the address above.

Slow The Fuck Down / Ashley Looker. —1st ed.
ISBN 978-1-953449-13-9

Dedicated to all the busy, ambitious, over-achieving perfectionists out there who are ready to put down the to-do list and pick up their life.

WELCOME, FRIEND

Do not confuse a busy life
with a purposeful one.
- Bob Goff

Nobody should be *this* busy. Nobody should be *this* overwhelmed. Nobody should be doing *this* much. As our schedules become fuller, time goes faster. As we continue to add more and more things to our to-do lists and schedules, the quicker the time passes. We keep getting more efficient and cutting more corners by life-hacking everything from meals to haircuts to vacations to exercise. And for what? To efficiently and 'perfectly' move through our lives? Sounds pretty boring to me.

Nearly every day we declare as if we have no control over what's happening, "Oh my gosh, time is just *flying* by!" Life is happening to us. We are so consumed with worry and stress that we rarely spend any time enjoying the present moment. Too many of us are living our lives driven by the misbelief that the more we do, the more valuable we are. Allow me to pause here and confirm, in case you are doubting your inherent worthiness, that this is complete and utter nonsense.

What's worse? When asked how we are doing, the response, as if a badge of honor, is always the same—our precious, sacred lives whittled down to one pathetic, lackluster word: *busy*.

Among all those misbeliefs and busyness is our careless disregard of simple pleasures. We believe that joy is some grandiose experience that, similar to that incredible romp with Javier in Cancun in 2001, only comes around every so often; and when it does, we cling to it, terrified for the joy to dissipate.

The truth is, joy isn't a rare occasion. We just aren't making it a priority.

Joy is a choice that we intentionally choose, practice and allow—like the hug we give our partner as they head out the door in the morning; the smell of the pine trees as you walk your neighborhood; the delicious, life-giving cup of coffee in our hand; or the way your child giggles to herself as she watches her favorite cartoon.

Unfortunately, we tend to see joy as frivolous. We command that we can 'rest when we're dead' and refuse to experience one moment of boredom. With every spare second we grab for our phones like junkies, desperately looking for that next hit of entertainment.

Joy is here, my friends, but we're missing it.

Why Am I Talking About This?

Unworthiness is an epidemic. And one of the ways we can overcome the hustle for our worthiness is by slowing the fuck down, having fun, and enjoying the present moment.

You see, if there were a winner in this *productivity = worthiness* shit-show we are living in, it'd be me. I would've done laps around your ass by now, and that's something I would have bragged about back in the day. Every ounce of my confidence, self-esteem, and worthiness was hung on my productivity like a very wet suit on a very slender man. But all that 'winning?' It came at a price. It came with meltdowns, anxiety attacks, never feeling good enough, resentment, angry outbursts 'for no reason', loneliness, and perfectionism.

I had been experiencing a nagging, desperate feeling for quite some time, but back then, who had time for that? Pay attention to thoughts and feelings!? Take something off my plate?! REST?! This literally sounded like my worst nightmare.

It wasn't until the fall of 2013 when my cousin asked me to try Bikram yoga that the tides of productivity and worth started to shift for me.

(Let it be noted that, of course, as a high-achieving, ambitious freak I had to do one of the most painstaking forms of yoga that existed because lord knows I couldn't let this journey be easy. Torturous yoga where I may pass out or puke? Sign. Me. Up.)

Shortly after starting to practice yoga, something interesting happened. I began noticing things. *Lots of things.* I started identifying feelings and thoughts more and more frequently, and those thoughts and feelings became little gold nuggets I'd explore in which I'd uncover wonderful little mysteries about myself. I started noticing how certain foods made my body feel. I started noticing my shitty thoughts and beliefs. I started noticing how certain people made me feel. And, most importantly, I started becoming aware of how my definition of a successful life was based solely on a standard and expectation that wasn't mine—a definition that was embedded in earning my worth, steeped in a lack of worthiness, and centered around hustling, proving myself, and chasing joy and success. Suddenly, everything started to make sense—and it was terrifying.

Had I really been chasing for years an idea of success that didn't really exist? Yes. And that, my friends, is why I'm here writing this book for you. It's a warning and a wake-up call.

Here's the thing: hustling is only *one* way to succeed. It's not the only way. And that's what you'll learn throughout this book. If you're cynical like me, we'll uncover lots of reasons why slowing down can improve your life. If you feel completely clueless and overwhelmed by the idea of slowing down, I'll provide lots of simple slowing-down ideas for you. And finally, as a yoga teacher (yeah, yoga and slowing down transformed my life so much that I decided to make it my career), I believe in the power of self-reflection and self-study. With each slowing-down concept you'll also be given a journaling prompt to explore your own relationship with busyness, productivity, and worthiness.

We hear stories like this all the time. The burned-out CEO gets in a car wreck where he almost loses his life and finally decides to go after his dream of becoming a business coach. Or the stressed-out mom loses her dad to diabetes and finally decides to take her own health into her hands by hiring a nanny one day a week so she can finally fucking rest. My hope is that by slowing down, and doing so now, we don't need something tragic to happen to finally wake up to the preciousness and sacredness of our lives. My hope is that by reading this and taking action, it'll inspire you to opt out—out of the competition, the chaos, the chase for more. So hold on tight, darling, it's going to be a very slooooow and intentional ride. ;)

Lastly, this book is largely based on personal experience. Resources and references are noted when available, but ultimately this book is me advocating through personal experience why slowing down is the answer to so many of our modern-day problems.

BEFORE WE BEGIN

What is your current relationship with busyness and productivity?
What ideally would you like for productivity to look and feel like?

_____

_____

_____

_____

_____

_____

_____

_____

_____

_____

_____

_____

_____

_____

_____

_____

_____

_____

_____

_____

1

LIFE ISN'T A COMPETITION
OR A RACE

Contrary to the bullshit we have all been fed, life is not a race nor is it a competition, although so much of our worthiness is dependent on winning. Barf. And as far as I know, there is no medal or prize for the person who gets to the end of their life the quickest, or makes the most money, or has the most followers on Instagram, or is the prettiest, or the most popular. And even if there was, is this a competition we want to win? *Or even care about?*

The only race you should be participating in is the one that gets you closest to your joy in the shortest amount of time. You do that, you definitely win.

Use the STOP method (stop, take three breaths, observe, proceed).

The moment you find yourself overwhelmed or stressed out, do this:

Stop. Literally. *Just stop.*
Take three deep breaths.
Observe how your body feels and see if you can identify any thoughts or feelings.
Proceed with compassion.

By keeping myself so busy, what am I distracting myself from?
What am I ignoring, avoiding or hiding from that needs my
attention?

_____

_____

_____

_____

_____

_____

_____

_____

_____

_____

_____

_____

_____

_____

_____

_____

_____

_____

_____

2

BEING BUSY AND HUSTLING DOESN'T MAKE YOU MORE VALUABLE OR WORTHY THAN YOU ALREADY ARE

The admiration of busyness and hustle is something that we have learned through our capitalistic society. The more we struggle, the better. The more we dis-trust ourselves and feel not good enough, the more we buy and consume in hopes of fixing our flaws. The harder we have to fight, "the bigger the success."

The truth is you could go through your entire life being absolutely perfect, checking every box, never making a mistake, and that perfection *still doesn't hold a candle to how worthy you already are.* Your worthiness is already decided, sweet cheeks. Your existence here on this earth means you are already worthy beyond anything that'll ever get checked off your to-do list.

Take one thing off your to-do list and replace it with joy.

There will always be another thing to do. If we keep putting off joy, for cleaning the oven or dusting the blinds (you know it's bad if you're dusting the blinds), we'll never experience the lives we were meant to live. You are worthy as fuck of your joy, and you're worthy of it right now. So put it on the list, boo!

What do I need to believe about myself and my worth to unhook from productivity and busyness as sources of my value?

_____

_____

_____

_____

_____

_____

_____

_____

_____

_____

_____

_____

_____

_____

_____

_____

_____

_____

_____

3

HAPPINESS IS CULTIVATED IN THE PRESENT MOMENT

I f you're hustling and bustling and rushing through life, it's damn near impossible to be in the present moment where happiness exists. When we are constantly worried about the future and what has to get done, we leave very, very little space for joy. Presence is your access point to your innate happiness.

Notice your 5 sensations.

We have these amazing senses that we rarely notice because we're too busy worrying about this, that, or the other thing. Today take a moment to notice what you see, feel, hear, smell, and taste. It will deepen your experience in your life and allow you to arrive in the present moment when, most likely, you've been thinking about the past or worrying about the future.

If I want to create the depth and connection with myself I truly desire, I will need to:

_____

_____

_____

_____

_____

_____

_____

_____

_____

_____

_____

_____

_____

_____

_____

_____

_____

_____

_____

_____

_____

4

RUSHING WON'T GET YOU "THERE" ANY FASTER

Contrary to what you may believe, rushing and hurrying toward a goal or outcome rarely gets you there any quicker than if you were to move slower and with more intention. If we use driving as an example, going 10 MPH over the speed limit for a 15-mile trip will only get you to your destination 2.5 minutes faster—a pretty sorry improvement, especially when you run the risk of getting into a wreck or getting a ticket. Don't lose the importance of how it feels on the journey toward your goal. If it feels like a fuck-ton of pressure, is the goal really worth it?

Center your day around a slow down intention or mantra.

Take a breath and ask yourself "How can I slow down today?" Whatever bubbles up for you, whether it be infusing more presence or kindness throughout your day or something else, formulate a mantra around it, write it down and say it to yourself throughout the day. Here are a couple examples I really love:

Slow is smooth and smooth is fast.
If I'm rushing, I'm missing it.
I choose to be intentional and present today.
Slowing down makes me more productive.

In what ways do I feel behind in my life? How do I know I'm behind? And what would it be like to know wholeheartedly that I am right on time?

_____

_____

_____

_____

_____

_____

_____

_____

_____

_____

_____

_____

_____

_____

_____

_____

_____

_____

_____

5

FASTER ISN'T ALWAYS BETTER,
I.E., QUALITY OVER QUANTITY

D o I love that I can order a new loveseat on Amazon and it could be here in two days? YES. However, when we move fast or production is increased, quality can be lost. The same goes for life. The faster we move, the more quality we can lose. To me, life is about the *depth* of experience, not the number of them we can tally up.

When you are out running errands, park far away and then walk slowly to your destination.

Power walking was for the 80's, friends.

Slowing down feels scary / hard / difficult because:

_____

_____

_____

_____

_____

_____

_____

_____

_____

_____

_____

_____

_____

_____

_____

_____

_____

_____

_____

_____

_____

_____

6

SPEEDING YOUR WAY THROUGH LIFE COULD BE CREATING STRESS IN YOUR BODY

(and possibly that mysterious stomach issue you've been dealing with for years)

Your body is like that really honest, overly assertive friend that is always "keepin' it real." Let's call her Sarah. Sarah will call you out on your bullshit to which you may say things like "you don't know what you're talking about!" or "whatever, Sarah," and brush it off.

Yet, the longer we ignore these messages, the louder Sarah (ahem, your body) gets. The next thing you know you get sick and can't get out of bed for four days. However, had you listened to Sarah a week ago you probably would have noticed those little sniffles and sore throat, ramped up your vitamin C intake, and gone to bed earlier.

Our bodies are always talking to us, and the busier we are, the more unconscious we are to its messages. When you stop living like a floating head and start tuning into your brilliant body, you'll create a relationship with it that will support your highest good in body, mind, and spirit.

Starfish on your floor for 5 minutes. *(My personal fave.)*

Lie on the floor with arms and legs wide like a big, beautiful starfish. Breathe. Feel the openness and expansion of your body. Feel your chest rise and fall. Let your body melt into the floor.

One belief that would support me in slowing down and being more mindful in my life is:

_____

_____

_____

_____

_____

_____

_____

_____

_____

_____

_____

_____

_____

_____

_____

_____

_____

_____

_____

_____

7

YOU'RE GONNA REGRET
MOVING SO FAST

Here's my biggest fear—that one day we all look back on our lives with regret that we didn't simply allow ourselves to lean into joy and fully enjoy our lives without the hustle, without the guilt, without the competition. You're going to want those moments back if you don't fully enjoy them, *so enjoy them now.*

Here's a quote to help you remember this one: "One day you'll look back on your life after all the pushing and striving and wonder why you didn't just allow yourself to be happy. Let yourself own your happiness now." - Danielle LaPorte

Say fuck off to the hustle.

Literally say this out loud right now. Say it loud and say it with gumption! Say it like you mean it! "FUCK THE HUSTLE!!" Feels good, doesn't it?

What do I not want to regret?

_____

_____

_____

_____

_____

_____

_____

_____

_____

_____

_____

_____

_____

_____

_____

_____

_____

_____

_____

_____

8

IDEAS GALORE!!

There is so much expansion in the present moment. Though it is fleeting, all possibility exists right now. When you slow down and allow yourself to bask in the present moment and let go of the outcomes, ideas flow in. Solutions to problems become clear and creativity ensues! It's rare that we can force ideas.

Slowing down is like turning on the faucet to our creativity! The slower we go and the more tuned in we are, the more ideas flow and more creative we become. And do you know what creativity and flow birth? You guessed it: joy.

Get caught up in being instead of doing.

Pump the fucking breaks, you beautiful, busy idiot. You may find that you are doing a lot right now. Pause. Take a beat to just *be* right now instead. Being is so much more powerful than doing because it doesn't matter *what* you're <u>doing</u> if *what* you're <u>being</u> is a dick.

What inessential and unimportant things can I eliminate from my life?

_____

_____

_____

_____

_____

_____

_____

_____

_____

_____

_____

_____

_____

_____

_____

_____

_____

_____

_____

_____

9

SLOWING DOWN WILL LESSEN YOUR ANXIETY

Slowing down asks us to be mindful. Mindfulness asks us to pay attention and notice. When we notice and observe, we are able to see what is creating and causing our stress and anxiety. And when we can identify a trigger, we can do something about it. And when we can do something about it, we feel safe. When we feel safe, we can relax. And when we are relaxed, we are in the relaxation response. And it's hard as hell to feel anxious when you're relaxed.

Instead of focusing on what you can get done, focus on how you want to feel.

This is a technique I adopted seven years ago from *The Desire Map* by Danielle LaPorte. She posits that when we ditch the to-do list with all those weighty obligations and instead design our days around how we want to feel, we are actually more productive. When you feel good, you're more inspired and energized. Give it a try! How do you want to feel today? Once you identify how you want to feel, make a list of the things you can do to feel that way. Then go do those things and see what happens!

What drama can I remove myself from today? What drama in my mind, circumstances, relationships, work, etc. can be eliminated?

_____

_____

_____

_____

_____

_____

_____

_____

_____

_____

_____

_____

_____

_____

_____

_____

_____

_____

_____

10

HUSTLE IS NOT A
RITE OF PASSAGE

There is nothing that says you have to walk over the fiery coals of hustle to be a successful adult. We all have busier seasons in our lives. Some are busy raising families and growing businesses, but hustle, which I directly associate with struggle, does not need to be a part of that story. There is nothing—I mean nothing—that says you have to hustle to be successful. There is nothing wrong with working your ass off, but you can work your ass off joyfully. Remember, hustling is only one way to succeed; *it's not the only way.*

Play. Have fun. *Go crazy.*

This is your permission slip to have fun. Fun doesn't feel very productive, does it? WHO CARES. The more fun you have, the happier you will be. Time spent happily is time well spent.

What would I love to be spending my time and energy on?

_____

_____

_____

_____

_____

_____

_____

_____

_____

_____

_____

_____

_____

_____

_____

_____

_____

_____

_____

_____

_____

11

CLEARER GUIDANCE AND CONNECTION TO YOUR INTUITION

When we are able to slow down and notice our thoughts and emotions, we are able to hear that little whisper of our intuition. Your intuition is your guidance system—not Tony Robbins, not Oprah, not me. When we slow down and listen to our intuition, we start to notice those gut feelings, those little synchronicities, those messages that are leading and guiding us through our lives.

Our intuition is our truth, and slowing down will allow you to access the truth and wisdom that is already within you. You don't need Google. You don't need to take a course on accessing your intuition. All you need to do is slow the fuck down.

Use a beginner's mind.

The first time you do anything is often an exceptional experience, right? And even if it isn't exceptional, we tend to remember the first time we do anything more vividly because it's new and exciting. Adopting a beginner's mindset will bring new light to your daily life. Go about your day as if you are experiencing it all for the first time. The walks, the cuddles, the cooking, the wind, the bath water, the smiles. See the miracles and magic happening around you. It's pretty incredible.

Right now my soul needs:

_____

_____

_____

_____

_____

_____

_____

_____

_____

_____

_____

_____

_____

_____

_____

_____

_____

_____

_____

_____

_____

12

YOU'LL DIGEST YOUR FOOD BETTER

Gassy? Bloated? Dealing with digestive discomfort? No, this is not a commercial for laxatives. This is your wake-up call!! The faster you eat, the more discomfort you will experience. I struggled with digestive issues for years, and once I started slowing down and being more mindful when I ate, my digestive issues reduced by about 40%. *40%!!* I didn't change what I ate, I changed *how* I ate. That's it. Plus, when we slow down during a meal we experience so much more pleasure. Eating is meant to be pleasurable, not a race.

Chew your food.

Many of us eat so quickly we give ourselves zero time to enjoy our amazing meals. Today, really chew your food and enjoy the fuck out of your meals.

Right now my body is telling me:

_____

_____

_____

_____

_____

_____

_____

_____

_____

_____

_____

_____

_____

_____

_____

_____

_____

_____

_____

_____

_____

_____

13

YOU CAN'T GET
IT BACK

Seems obvious enough, but not enough for us to slow the fuck down, now does it? You will never get this moment back. Do you really want to miss more precious moments? Didn't think so. Now that we know better, let's do better.

Savor something.

A meal, a kiss, a smile, a song, a dance, a laugh, the rain, sunset, cuddles with your dog. Savor it. Soak it up. Let it land in your body and soul. Savoring the moments is what life is all about and it's also been proven to increase your happiness.

In what ways are busyness and my need for productivity holding me back from being my best self, living my best life, and displaying my best qualities?

_____

_____

_____

_____

_____

_____

_____

_____

_____

_____

_____

_____

_____

_____

_____

_____

_____

_____

_____

14

SLOW DOWN YOUR BREATH,
SLOW DOWN YOUR MIND

Trust me, I'm a busy, ambitious, Type A, overachieving, recovering perfectionist who constantly has something on her mind. The majority of us breathe shallowly and quickly which can provoke anxiety. When we slow down our breath, the mind often follows. Give it a try with the belly breathing technique outlined below.

Practice belly breathing.

Breathing into your belly sends a message to your brain that you are safe and that you can relax. Take a moment to just notice the breath. Notice where it is showing up for you and how it feels. Then, on your next inhale, breathe in through the nose, dragging the breath deep into the lungs and all the way down into the belly.

Allow the belly and lower ribs to expand outward, ballooning the belly. Then slowly exhale the breath out through the nose until you are completely empty of air. Repeat three more times and as frequently as possible.

How am I making things harder on myself than they need to be?

_____

_____

_____

_____

_____

_____

_____

_____

_____

_____

_____

_____

_____

_____

_____

_____

_____

_____

_____

_____

_____

15

DEEPEN LOVE AND CONNECTION WITHIN YOUR RELATIONSHIPS

Instead of running around like a chicken with your head cut off the majority of the day, slow down and nurture your relationships and your life. Talk—and actually listen. Make eye contact for fuck sake, and get off your phone. That little rectangle is a life-suck, zapping precious time and energy that you will never get back.

When you're grabbing drinks with friends, stop worrying about what your hair looks like, stop worrying about what time you need to leave, stop rushing. Just STOP. Time with your loved ones is precious. Don't ruin it by constantly worrying or being distracted by Instagram. Be present with them. It's one of the most precious gifts we can give ourselves and others.

Sign this commitment:

Today I am committing to slowing the fuck down. Today I wholeheartedly understand that my joy is 1,000 times more important than getting a new lamp at Target. Starting today I will not forsake my joy or sacrifice my needs to please or impress someone else or check another thing off my list. I sign this today with gusto and permission to live my life differently, deeply, and aligned with my joy.

How can I make space for creativity, art, beauty, and play today?

_____
_____
_____
_____
_____
_____
_____
_____
_____
_____
_____
_____
_____
_____
_____
_____
_____
_____
_____
_____
_____

16

YOU'LL CONNECT DEEPER WITH
YOUR LIFE PURPOSE

I want to suggest something that may feel radically different from how you've lived your life. That is: joy is your purpose. It's not to become a doctor or win that hotdog eating contest. I believe that our purpose is to be who we authentically are and doing so creates meaning and purpose in our lives. Our occupation is only one way we can express and experience our joy. It's not the end all be all. And as you may have guessed, this takes slowing down, checking in with yourself and asking, am I being who I want to be right now? Am I aligned with my integrity and values? The more aligned we are, the more purposeful (and joyful) we feel.

Life Inventory: Romance, Family / Friends, Career, Money, Creativity / Play, Spirituality, Health / Wellbeing, Environment.

Take a loving look at these areas of your life. Are you in alignment with your values, your authenticity, and your joy in each of these areas? If so, great! If not, take some time today to come up with ideas that would inch you closer to your authenticity, purpose, and joy in these areas. Notice how I didn't say "come up with the perfect way to be in perfect integrity and joy in these areas." Yeah, you might fall short in some categories, but aiming for perfection won't help you here because it doesn't exist.

How can I create a deeper sense of purpose (ahem, joy) in my life today?

_____

_____

_____

_____

_____

_____

_____

_____

_____

_____

_____

_____

_____

_____

_____

_____

_____

_____

17

WHEN YOU SLOW THE FUCK DOWN, YOU'LL GET TO KNOW YOURSELF BETTER

When you slow down and pay attention, you'll start to notice really amazing things like:

Sweet potatoes actually hurt your stomach.
Your energy really plummets around 2 p.m.
You're really annoyed by your complaining lately.
You're most energized in the early morning.
You're really comparing yourself to Lisa lately.
You noticed a pang of jealousy last night when you saw how cute and lovey Brett and Kelly looked together.

All of these things are invitations to explore yourself and get to know yourself better (not to beat yourself up for having a human experience). And when we know ourselves, we can give ourselves what we need and want. Now that's empowerment!

Schedule 15 minutes to read an actual book simply for joy and pleasure.

Put down the self-help, darling. Take your busy brain offline for 15 minutes and enjoy the shenanigans of a raunchy novel. You won't regret it.

How would I be showing up differently in my life, my business, my relationships if I were unapologetic about what I wanted and needed?

_____

_____

_____

_____

_____

_____

_____

_____

_____

_____

_____

_____

_____

_____

_____

_____

_____

_____

_____

_____

18

NO MO' FOMO

When you slow down and honor where you are in your life and give yourself what you need, my hunch is that you will have less FOMO—fear of missing out. That party you want to go to or that course you want to take? You'll have less anxiety about missing out because you'll trust that the opportunities you desire won't miss you. You'll trust your decisions because they will be intentional rather than unconscious.

Get in the bath without your phone.

Listen, if you have your phone in hand, you're most likely unconscious and numbed out, scrolling and scrolling, which means you're missing the warmth of the water, the smell of the candle, the feeling of your body, the joy of the present moment. Quite literally, you're missing the experience. And for what?

Give it a try and see what you notice! (And don't worry—you won't miss out on anything as important as this moment.)

What stories am I telling myself that are holding me back?

_____
_____
_____
_____
_____
_____
_____
_____
_____
_____
_____
_____
_____
_____
_____
_____
_____
_____
_____
_____
_____
_____

19

SPONTANEOUS, QUICK DECISIONS ARE FUN, *BUUUT* CAN LAND YOU IN TROUBLE WITH YOUR PARTNER (OR IN JAIL)

That tattoo in Tijuana? That one-night stand? That project at work you said yes to that you really didn't want to take on but felt rushed and obligated? When you slow down and take your time with your decisions, you tend to make the decision that is right for you and your highest good. That dragon tattoo may have felt like a good idea at the moment, but the morning after? Not so much.

Downshift your thinking.

If you find yourself in an overwhelmed moment, don't worry. Think about what it would be like to downshift your thinking just like you would downshift a car.

I'll sometimes tell myself "slow down, sister"—something I learned from Gabby Bernstein. Take a moment to get curious and see if you can notice the thoughts that are coming up. Noticing the thoughts allows us to catch up with them so we can change them.

If I took things patiently, step by step, what could I conquer and accomplish?

_____

_____

_____

_____

_____

_____

_____

_____

_____

_____

_____

_____

_____

_____

_____

_____

_____

_____

_____

_____

20

NOTHING IS THAT URGENT

Unless your life is at risk, I would bet that nothing is as urgent as it's made out to be. The deadline, being late, the to-do list, the errands . . . IT AIN'T URGENT. Yeah I mean, don't be a dick and disrespect people's time, but life is not an emergency, people! Slow your roll and know damn near nothing is *that* urgent.

Schedule in non-structured time (or a day of nothing).

Did you just have a mini-pani? Don't panic, my love. Having nothing on your schedule gives you the openness, spaciousness, expansion, and freedom from that rigid schedule that you've been craving. Stop suffocating your joy with all that scheduled time. It's time to come up for air.

What is the harder choice that I have been avoiding?

_____

_____

_____

_____

_____

_____

_____

_____

_____

_____

_____

_____

_____

_____

_____

_____

_____

_____

_____

_____

_____

_____

21

MORE RESPONDING, LESS REACTING

Y ou fly off the handle at your partner, kids, or coworker and holy crap do you feel bad afterward. Then, to make matters worse, you guilt yourself, beat yourself up, and wish you could take it back. We've all been there. But how would it feel if this happened less and less? The more space we create between the stimulus and the response (partner says something dumb → you react by calling him a dumbass), the less likely we are to fall victim to a default, automatic reaction. As a bonus, this ultimately saves us from saying a bunch of stuff we probably didn't mean.

Use the R.A.I.N. Method: recognize, allow, investigate, nurture.

1. Recognize the emotion, feeling, thought, or sensation coming up for you.
2. Allow whatever is coming up for you to come through. Process it, experience it, give yourself a moment to be with it.
3. Investigate what potentially triggered the emotion / experience. Get curious about it. Lean in. The more you learn about it, the better you will be able to address it next time.
4. Nurture yourself with kindness and compassion moving forward.

If I were to lead with love and compassion today instead of hustle, productivity, and scarcity, I would:

_____
_____
_____
_____
_____
_____
_____
_____
_____
_____
_____
_____
_____
_____
_____
_____
_____
_____
_____
_____

22

LESS IMPULSE BUYS (AND MORE MONEY SAVED—*CHA-CHING!*)

I see you over there with $286 worth of things in your Amazon cart. Hold the phone, baby doll! Before you hit that one-click buy, ask yourself, *Do I really need these things or is this just some quick way to "fix" my sadness or fill a void where I'm feeling empty?*

The more we slow down and check in with our intentions for consumption, the more we may realize we just don't need the thing as badly as we thought. Oftentimes when we are tempted to buy something, it's an attempt to make us happy when what we really need is something much deeper (and often free) like a hug, a walk, or a loving conversation.

Tap out of the competition.

Instead of double-tapping that perfect picture of perfect Sarah with her perfect family on Instagram, double-tap your way right out of the comparison and competition by getting off or drastically reducing your time spent on social media. Sometimes social media can feel like a beauty contest or a race to show how happy and perfect and adventurous everyone's life is. Life is not a popularity contest and has nothing to do with your joy.

What could I stand to simplify or pare down in my life for the sake of my sanity?

_____

_____

_____

_____

_____

_____

_____

_____

_____

_____

_____

_____

_____

_____

_____

_____

_____

_____

23

LESS JUDGMENT,
MORE EMPATHY

In full transparency, I can be a judgmental asshole. As a recovering perfectionist and productivity junkie, one of my default patterns over the years has been to be hyper-critical and judgmental about my progress, my success, my creativity, my relationships, and so on. When I am able to s-l-o-w down my thoughts (using many of the techniques outlined in this book), I shift out of the judgment and into curiosity, compassion, and understanding. And guess what? Being compassionate and understanding will get you so much closer to your goals and your joy than judgment ever will.

I can't write a book about joy and slowing down without mentioning gratitude. **Practicing gratitude can change your entire outlook.** It's the ultimate attitude adjustment. It will literally rewire your brain for happiness.

The simple act of writing down what you are grateful for or expressing gratitude verbally has the potential to increase your happiness levels exponentially. Suffice it to say, if you do one thing from this book that will increase your happiness, *this is it.* This is what I would recommend.

The new principles, guideposts, and values that will govern my behavior moving forward are:

_____

_____

_____

_____

_____

_____

_____

_____

_____

_____

_____

_____

_____

_____

_____

_____

_____

_____

_____

_____

_____

24

IT'LL START TO BECOME INCREASINGLY CLEAR WHAT *REALLY* MATTERS IN YOUR LIFE

And it's not that Instagram post. I promise. I've spent an absurd amount of time fixing filters for social media. It's actually quite embarrassing. But it all came to a head one day when I dropped an entire container of spinach on my kitchen floor and my first reaction was to grab my phone and post about it. RED. FUCKING. FLAG.

Why on earth would I think people would want to see this? What's so important about this that it would need to be shared with the world? Because of social media, what we've deemed important has become completely skewed.

The truth of the matter is this: I'd much rather spend the next 20 minutes of my life looking into the eyes of my loved one or writing a page of my book (yep, *this one*) than fix a filter on a post. You feel me?

Write someone a handwritten letter.

Yes, you could send a nice text to your friend in about 15.3 seconds. But you wanna know what'll really hit her in her heart? A thoughtful, handwritten letter that took real time and effort. It'll show that you really care and no doubt it'll make someone's freaking day, including your own.

What kind of person am I going to decide to be today?

_____
_____
_____
_____
_____
_____
_____
_____
_____
_____
_____
_____
_____
_____
_____
_____
_____
_____
_____
_____
_____
_____
_____

25

LESS ACCIDENTS

Cut yourself with a knife because you're chopping those potatoes like a chef on Chopped? Forgot to put the car in park before you jumped out? Accidentally back into a light post because you're late picking up the kids? Or, worse, spill your full cup of delicious coffee all over your favorite band t-shirt as you're rushing out the door? Okay, maybe that's just *my* worst kind of accident, but I digress. Point is, slowing down has the potential to save us from a lot of unfortunate accidents. Slow is smooth.

Slow goodbyes and slow hellos.

We say goodbye and hello so many times throughout the day—at the grocery store, gas station, at home, on the street. Today, slow them down. Savor the conversation, the eye contact, the feeling, the moment. Let it mean more than just words. *Experience it.*

What do I keep doing in my life even though I hate it?

_____

_____

_____

_____

_____

_____

_____

_____

_____

_____

_____

_____

_____

_____

_____

_____

_____

_____

_____

26

WHERE'D I PUT MY KEYS?

O h, the age-old question. When you slow down and are mindful and present, you're much more likely to remember whether or not you turned your curling iron off before leaving the house. This, in turn, can potentially save you 10.2 hours of your life (a guesstimate of time I've personally wasted) because you will no longer need to turn around and go back home every time you fear you're gonna burn your house down from a curling iron fire.

You'll also remember where you put your keys—or your phone.

Take two minutes to see how still you can get your mind and body.

It's a mini slow-down challenge!

What would it look like if I 100% trusted myself and knew, no matter what, everything would be okay?

_____

_____

_____

_____

_____

_____

_____

_____

_____

_____

_____

_____

_____

_____

_____

_____

_____

_____

27

YOU'LL RECOGNIZE YOUR RESISTANCE AND BE MORE COURAGEOUS

For so many years, I allowed fear to stop me dead in my tracks (and, let's be honest, sometimes it still does). The slight feeling of fear and resistance sent me crying back to my comfort zone. By slowing down and building a relationship with fear and resistance, you'll start to understand it and create a new default pattern that aligns with courage. You'll no longer let fear and resistance dictate your decisions. You only need 20 seconds of courage to change the outcome of a situation.

Take a nap.

('cause you're gonna need it after being so brave all the time ;))

If my success wasn't attached to my productivity, my to-do list, the money in my bank, or how burned out and exhausted I was, I would measure my success by:

_____

_____

_____

_____

_____

_____

_____

_____

_____

_____

_____

_____

_____

_____

_____

_____

_____

_____

_____

28

YOU'LL CREATE A DEEPER SENSE OF CONNECTION WITH THE UNIVERSE, NATURE, YOUR SOUL, AND YOUR SENSES

The world is full of possibility, potential, ideas, beauty, opportunity, and joy. When we slow down long enough to pay attention, we start to notice all the little details in life that are so beautiful. The sights, the smells, the sounds! We begin to really understand, see, and feel with an open heart how connected everyone and everything is. Nothing is better or worse than the next thing. Nothing is further along or behind. There is no rush. Nothing you say or do will get you to where you want to go quicker than you are meant to. I know. How annoying. Yet, what a relief.

Joy exists in our spiritual DNA, which is exactly why we can be surprised by joy in the most ordinary moments. It's why, when you are having the crappiest of crappy days, the smell of freshly baked biscuits as you walk through the door can bring a smile to your face. These tiny precious moments are the ones we often miss but that make life exponentially better.

Today, participate in an embodiment practice.

Dance, adorn yourself with amazing jewelry or clothes you feel oh-so-good in, get a massage, look at beautiful art, express yourself creatively, listen to music, tap into your sensuality, do yoga, have sex. Embodiment practices nourish our souls and fill us up on a level that food and things never could.

What lessons did I come to this earth to learn?

_____
_____
_____
_____
_____
_____
_____
_____
_____
_____
_____
_____
_____
_____
_____
_____
_____
_____
_____
_____
_____
_____

29

INCREASED CONFIDENCE

I think we've all agreed by now that the present moment is the most powerful moment. The more present you are, the more powerful you feel. And the more powerful you feel, my hunch is, the more confident you will become—at least, this was the case for me and many of my clients. And if it could work, why not try it?

Confidence isn't found in a diet, a compliment, likes, followers, or a promotion because all of those things are temporary and exist outside of yourself. The moment you stop depending on those things to feel good about yourself is the moment you get your power back. Confidence is generated from within by knowing who you are and recognizing once and for all what a badass you are.

Carve out 10 minutes to write a list of all the things within you that cultivate confidence.

Then, make another list of all the things that rip your confidence away. Match them up. For example, let's say one thing that rips away your confidence is comparing yourself to Kelly, the amazing fitness trainer with thousands of followers, yet one thing that boosts your confidence is moving your body in a way that feels so good. Match them. Then, the next time you find yourself comparing yourself to Kelly, you can move your body in whatever way is calling you in the moment.

I am an empowered human. Today I choose...

_____

_____

_____

_____

_____

_____

_____

_____

_____

_____

_____

_____

_____

_____

_____

_____

_____

_____

_____

_____

_____

_____

30

YOUR LIFE MATTERS
AND YOU SHOULD
TAKE IT SERIOUSLY

Every a-ha moment, every cheesy smile, every breath, every conversation, every smell, sound, sight, touch, experience—everything is sacred and meant for you. Don't miss it! This life you've been given has so many beautiful things to offer you if you just slow down and notice. It matters, it counts, it's important. You life has meaning, it has value.

Be IN your life, because that truly is the only way to live a fulfilling life.

Throw yourself a celebration!!

Cue the confetti! Hang the streamers! Get out the fine china! Unleash the stampede of puppies!

It's time to revel in your life. Look around wherever you are and notice all the amazing things. This life is for you, no one else. It's yours. And it deserves a celebration! Today, slow down and celebrate your one sacred life.

What happiness have I been putting off for the sake of productivity that I can actually have right now?

_____
_____
_____
_____
_____
_____
_____
_____
_____
_____
_____
_____
_____
_____
_____
_____
_____
_____
_____
_____
_____

Made in the USA
Monee, IL
22 March 2021

62737216R00039